SEP 1 2 2006

E J

21891

Johnson
Who's upside down?

WHO'S UPSIDE DOWN?

Who's Upside Down?

WORDS AND PICTURES BY

Crockett Johnson

Linnet Books / Hamden, Connecticut

Published 1990 as a Linnet Book,
an imprint of The Shoe String Press, Inc.
Hamden, Connecticut 06514.
First published 1952 by William R. Scott, Inc.

Library of Congress Cataloging in Publication Data

Johnson, Crockett, 1906–

Who's upside down? / words and pictures
by Crockett Johnson.
        p.   cm.
"First published 1952 by William R. Scott, Inc."
—T.p. verso.

Summary: A kangaroo in Australia studies a picture
of the earth in a geography book and decides she must
be upside down.
[1. Kangaroos—Fiction.   2. Geography—Fiction.
3. Humorous stories.   4. Gravity—Fiction.]   I. Title.
PZ7.J63162Wh   1990
[Fic]—dc20
ISBN 0-208-02276-7 (alk. paper)

The paper in this publication meets the minimum requirements
of American National Standard for Information Sciences
— Permanence of Paper for Printed Library Materials,
ANSI Z 39.48–1984. ⊗

Printed in the United States of America

WHO'S UPSIDE DOWN?

Halfway around the world from you, a kangaroo was hopping up and down, the way kangaroos hop when everything seems to be perfectly right. A clear high sky rose above her head, and the hill beneath her feet was covered with grass that was tasty and tender.

She smiled down at her little kangaroo who was sleeping peacefully.

"Everything," she said, "is right in its place. And I am on top of the world."

She hopped up and down, looking for the very tenderest grass, tasting a tuft here, munching a few blades there. But suddenly she stopped.

There on the grass was a book.

It must have dropped down there on the grass when it slipped from the fingers of somebody who was taking the long way home from school or from the library. Such a thing happens now and then; it can happen to anybody.

"What's this?" said the kangaroo, staring at the book, sniffing at it, and wondering.

She picked up the book, which was open at a picture of the world. This was not so surprising because it happened to be a geography book.

"The world," said the kangaroo, staring, "looks like a big ball."

It did look like a big ball in the picture because the world *is* a big ball and this was an excellent picture of it, full of remarkable detail. In the picture the kangaroo saw you, standing around where you live and not doing anything very much at the moment, and, halfway around the world, there was she.

"Oh!" cried the kangaroo who had been feeling on top of the world until she saw herself in the picture. "I'm down underneath! And upside down!"

She couldn't really believe it at first. She looked again. Then she slowly said:

"It certainly seems to be so!"

When a thing *seems* to be so, kangaroos usually hop to the conclusion that it *is* so. She believed she was upside down.

And once she really believed it, she began to *feel* upside down.

Now, on the next page of that book was a picture of the world with pointers on it and words that read:

"Important Notice. People and animals who have their feet on the ground any place in the world are not upside down, no matter how they seem to be in this picture. And it is ridiculous for them to feel upside down. Quite ridiculous. Read the pointers. *Down* is down to earth, the way things go when they slip out of your hand, or the way you go when you fall down. *Up* is up the other way."

But the kangaroo couldn't read, even very short words. And she did feel upside down.

She felt very upside down indeed.

She hopped up and down, the way kangaroos hop when everything seems to be perfectly wrong. But she suddenly stopped when she thought:

"Oh, I'm not hopping up and down at all! I'm hopping *down* and *up!*"

And the thought that she was looking *down* at the sky and gazing *up* at the grass made her sob.

She was very upset.

She sobbed so hard the little kangaroo woke up, wondering what in the world the trouble was.

"Your mother," she wailed, "is upside down!"

The little kangaroo hopped to the ground, stepped back, and looked at the big kangaroo.

"You look all right to me, ma."

"That's because you're upside down too!" sobbed the big kangaroo, holding out the book. "Everything around here is upside down! See?"

"Everything?" The little kangaroo, who couldn't read either, stood frowning at the picture, tipping the book to one side or the other. "Then the book is upside down too, isn't it?"

"Everything," said the big kangaroo. "*Everything* is upside down! And we can't do a thing about it."

"At least we can turn the book around," said the little kangaroo.

Suddenly the little kangaroo laughed and hopped back to the big kangaroo's lap, humming a carefree song that went something like, "Mother kangaroos have laps they don't lose, and their children hop into them whenever they choose," or, anyway, the *tune* seemed to be to that effect.

The little kangaroo held the book up before the mother kangaroo's tear-filled eyes.

And the way the little kangaroo held it now, the picture of the world was turned around.

The big kangaroo looked at the picture of the world and she blinked.

She looked around her. She looked *up* at the sky, and *down* at the grass-covered hill.

Her eyes opened wide. She smiled.

She hopped. She hopped *up* and then *down*.

Everything seemed to be right in its place and she felt on top of the world. But she looked at the book again to be sure.

"I *am* on top of the world," she said.

The little kangaroo went back to sleep. And the big kangaroo once more began to hop up and down, the way kangaroos hop when everything seems to be perfectly right.

She has felt all right ever since. But, now and then, she feels a little bit sad, because she thinks

YOU are upside down.

CROCKETT JOHNSON

About the Author . . .

Crockett Johnson was born David Johnson Leisk in New York City in 1906, was educated at Cooper Union and New York University, and was the husband of children's author Ruth Krauss. Creator of the comic strip "Barnaby," which syndicated for over twenty years, Johnson was also author-illustrator of some twenty books for children and illustrator of an additional eight.

Perhaps the most well known of Crockett Johnson's books is *Harold and the Purple Crayon,* a simple story in which Harold uses his purple crayon to create his own adventures — drawing his way from page to page until he closes his day by drawing his own bed and climbing in.

Who's Upside Down? shares the same whimsicality as this and subsequent *Harold* books. Published originally in 1952 by William R. Scott, *Who's Upside Down?* tackles the question of gravity in a few simple words and, as the *New York Times* observed at that time, "Children will be delighted."